Stories of GREAT PEOPLE

Mozart's wig

Gerry Bailey and Karen Foster

Illustrated by Leighton Noyes
and Karen Radford

🌣 Crabtree Publishing Company

www.crabtreebooks.com

HANNAH PLATT is Digby's argumentative, older sister—and she doesn't believe a word that *Mr. Rummage* says!

DIGBY PLATT is an antique collector. Every Saturday he picks up a bargain at *Mr. Rummage's* antique stall and loves listening to the story behind his new 'find'.

Mr. RUMMAGE has a stall piled high with interesting objects—and he has a great story to tell about each and every one of his treasures.

CHRISSY's vintage clothing stall has all the costumes Digby and Hannah need to act out the characters in Mr. Rummage's stories.

KENZO the barber has a wig for every occasion, and is always happy to put his scissors to use!

Crabtree Publishing Company

www.crabtreebooks.com

Other books in the series

Armstrong's moon rock

Cleopatra's coin

Columbus's chart

Galileo's telescope

Julius Caesar's sandals

Leonardo's palette

Marco Polo's silk purse

Martin Luther King Jr.'s microphone

Mother Teresa's alms bowl

Queen Victoria's diamond

Shakespeare's quill

Sitting Bull's tomahawk

The Wright Brothers' glider

Credits

AKG Images: p. 13 (bottom left), 18 (bottom), 21 (bottom), 22; Erich Lessing: p. 25 (bottom left); Erich Lessing/Kunsthistorisches, Vienna: p. 18 (top), 24; Erich Lessing/Mozart Museum, Salzburg: p. 9, 10 (top right), 35; Erich Lessing/Musée Condé, Chantilly: p. 13 (top right); Erich Lessing/Schloss Schoenbrunn, Vienna: p. 13 (bottom right), 21 (top); Museum Narodowe, Warsaw: p. 17 (bottom left); Staatliche Preussischer Kulturbesitz, Berlin: p. 10 (center); Tretjakov Gallery, Moscow: p. 27 (bottom right)
Private Collection/Bridgeman Art Library: p. 10 (bottom left)
Lebrecht Music & Arts: p. 27 (top right), 28 (bottom right), 31, 32 (bottom right); Private Collection: p. 27 (bottom left)
Mary Evans Picture Library: p. 25 (top and bottom right), 28 (top), 32 (top right)

Picture research: Diana Morris. info@picture-research.co.uk
Editor: Lynn Peppas
Proofreaders: David Hurd, Crystal Sikkens
Project editor: Robert Walker
Prepress technician: Ken Wright
Production coordinator: Margaret Amy Salter

Library and Archives Canada Cataloguing in Publication

Bailey, Gerry
    Mozart's wig / Gerry Bailey and Karen Foster ; illustrated by Leighton Noyes and Karen Radford.

(Stories of great people)
Includes index.
ISBN 978-0-7787-3696-7 (bound).--ISBN 978-0-7787-3718-6 (pbk.)

    1. Mozart, Wolfgang Amadeus, 1756-1791--Juvenile fiction. 2. Composers--Austria--Biography--Juvenile fiction. 3. Mozart, Wolfgang Amadeus, 1756-1791--Juvenile literature. 4. Composers--Austria--Biography--Juvenile literature. I. Noyes, Leighton II. Radford, Karen III. Foster, Karen, 1959- IV. Title. V. Series.

PZ7.B15Mo 2008   j823'.92   C2008-907027-5

Library of Congress Cataloging-in-Publication Data

Bailey, Gerry.
  Mozart's wig / Gerry Bailey and Karen Foster ; illustrated by Leighton Noyes and Karen Radford.
      p. cm. -- (Stories of great people)
  Includes index.
  ISBN 978-0-7787-3718-6 (pbk. : alk. paper) -- ISBN 978-0-7787-3696-7 (reinforced library binding : alk. paper)
  1. Mozart, Wolfgang Amadeus, 1756-1791--Juvenile literature. 2. Composers--Austria--Biography--Juvenile literature. I. Foster, Karen, 1959- II. Noyes, Leighton, ill. III. Radford, Karen, ill. IV. Title. V. Series.

ML3930.M9B23 2009
780.92--dc22
[B]
                                            2008046282

Crabtree Publishing Company

www.crabtreebooks.com   1-800-387-7650

Published in Canada
Crabtree Publishing
616 Welland Ave.
St. Catharines, Ontario
L2M 5V6

Published in the United States
Crabtree Publishing
PMB16A
350 Fifth Ave., Suite 3308
New York, NY 10118

Published by CRABTREE PUBLISHING COMPANY
Copyright © **2009** Diverta Ltd.

Mozart's wig
Table of Contents

Every Saturday morning, Knicknack Market comes to life. The street vendors are there almost before the sun is up. And by the time you and I are out of bed, the stalls are built, the boxes are opened, and all the goods are carefully laid out on display.

Objects are piled high. Some are laid out on velvet: precious necklaces and jeweled swords. Others stand upright at the back: large, framed pictures of very important people, lamps made from tasseled satin, and old-fashioned cash registers—the kind that jingle when the drawers are opened. And then there are things that stay in their boxes all day, waiting for the right customer to come along: war medals laid out in straight lines, stopwatches on leather straps, and utensils in polished silver for all those special occasions.

But Mr. Rummage's stall is different. Mr. Rummage of Knicknack Market has a stall piled high with a disorderly jumble of things that no one could ever want.

Who'd want to buy a stuffed mouse? Or a broken umbrella? Or a pair of false teeth?

Well, Mr. Rummage has them all. And, as you can imagine, they don't cost a lot!

Digby Platt—ten-year-old collector of antiques—was off to see his friend Mr. Rummage of Knicknack Market.

It was Saturday and, as usual, Digby's weekly allowance was burning a hole in his pocket.

Digby wasn't going to spend it on any old thing. It had to be something rare and interesting for his collection, something from Mr. Rummage's incredible stall.

Hannah, his older sister, had come along as usual. She had secret doubts about the value of Mr. Rummage's objects and felt, for some big-sisterly reason, that she had to stop her little brother from buying useless junk.

"Well, look who's here," said Mr. Rummage, "happily, my two favorite customers."

"Hi, Mr. Rummage," said Digby, "What's new?"

"Nothing," said Mr. Rummage, "it's all old. That's why it's an antiques stall."

Digby laughed. "Even that old bit of hair?" he said pointing to a strange looking wig.

"Don't be disgusting," said Hannah. "It's probably some kind of wig."

"You're right, Hannah," replied Mr. Rummage. "That wig belonged to the greatest musician of all time."

"Elvis Presley!" exclaimed Digby.

"Mr. Rummage," someone interrupted. "Your young customer seems to be a bit of a comedian." It was Kenzo the barber, who'd popped over at the mention of the word—wig. "No, young man. That's got to be Mozart's wig."

"It is." began Mr. Rummage. Kenzo ignored Mr. Rummage and continued, "But in those day's—over 300 years ago in the 1700's—almost anybody

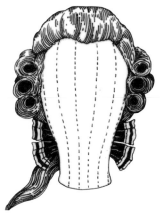

who was anybody wore a wig. They were made of real hair—not human hair, but horsehair. They were perfumed and powdered, and some were tied behind with velvet bows. Anyway, they were shaped on carved stands and styled with **pomades**, and really wealthy people would have a wig for every occasion. Those were the days when hairdressers like me were very important people indeed."

"Are you quite sure this Mozart wore one?" asked Hannah suspiciously. "And what's it doing here?"

"Mozart was a child **prodigy**," declared Mr. Rummage, choosing to ignore Hannah's second question, "who became one of the world's greatest composers, although not everyone recognized this at the time."

Wolfgang Amadeus Mozart

Wolfgang Amadeus Mozart was born above a shop in the Austrian city of Salzburg on January 27, 1756. He was christened Joannes Christosomos Wolfgang Theophilus. Theophilus means "beloved of God," which is "Amadeus" in Latin–so he became known as Wolfgang Amadeus. To confuse things even more, his parents called him by the pet names "Woferl" or "Wolfgangerl."

Wolfgang's parents were Leopold, a talented musician and **composer**, and Anna Maria Pertl. He also had a sister, Maria Anna, or "Nannerl" for short. Leopold soon discovered that both his children were gifted musicians, especially young Wolfgang. The boy was able to compose beautiful music from a very young age and went on to produce a huge amount of work in a very short lifetime.

Let's find out more...

Early years

A family business

Leopold was a strict but loving father who gave up his career to educate and promote his children. Some people think he just used their talent to make money, but that would be unfair. He really cared for them and wanted the best for them. Leopold was strict, but Wolfgang was very close to his father and wanted to please him. He loved his mother too, although she stayed at home and only traveled with the children once. His letters home are always full of kisses for her.

First concerto

Wolfgang enjoyed life and was full of fun and mischief. He wrote all over chairs and tables and even the floor. At the age of four he began butting in on his sister Nannerl's **harpsichord** lessons, so Leopold decided to teach them together. Wolfgang made rapid progress and soon overtook his talented sister. He even tried to compose little **duets** they could play together. One day Leopold came home to find Wolfgang scribbling away. When the boy handed him a piece of paper smudged with notes and ink-blots, he laughed. But then Leopold saw the important part—the music—and burst into tears of joy and wonder. Wolfgang had written the first part of a "**concerto**."

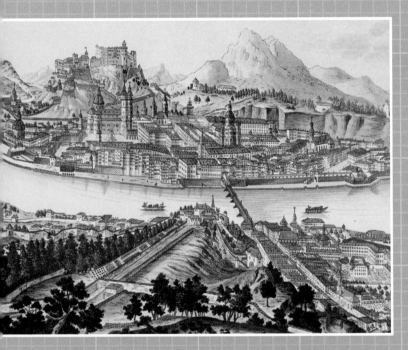

WOLFGANG WAS BROUGHT UP IN SALZBURG, A TINY CITY-STATE AT THAT TIME, WEDGED IN BETWEEN THE EUROPEAN COUNTRIES OF AUSTRIA AND BAVARIA.

"Such a brilliant boy," sighed Kenzo. "Everyone loved him. He was so cute."

"He was," continued Mr. Rummage. "Imagine... when he was only three he'd pick out notes on the **clavier**—that's a kind of piano—while his sister practiced."

"They called her Nannerl," said Kenzo, "wasn't that charming?"

"Er, yes. Very charming," said Mr. Rummage. "Anyway, Wolfgang loved the sound of the piano and by the age of five he was learning and playing complete pieces."

"Wow, he must have been good," said Digby.

"He was, but he had one particular gift that helped a great deal. Wolfgang had a fantastic memory. He could remember a piece after listening to it just once, and then play it off by heart."

"So he had a kind of photographic memory?" suggested Hannah.

"Yes," said Mr. Rummage. "In fact he used to say that whenever he composed he could hear the music in his head: he'd hear all the parts for all the instruments, and when he'd imagined the whole piece, he'd write it all down.

Once his father saw how talented he was, he concentrated all his effort on helping Wolfgang develop."

"Was he one of those pushy parents who pressure their children?" asked Hannah.

"Not really," replied Mr. Rummage, "although he did expect both his children to work hard. They'd have lessons during the day and then play together or invite friends over in the drawing room in the evening."

"I wouldn't call that pushy," said Digby. "I'd call it fun!"

"Was he on the radio?" asked Digby. Hannah screeched with laughter. "They didn't have radios in those days, silly. We're talking over two hundred years ago."

"No indeed," said Mr. Rummage, "but by the time Wolfgang was six, Leopold wanted to show off his children to the rest of the world. That meant traveling, so he took them to the German city of Munich and presented them at the splendid court of the ruler of Bavaria."

"Were they a success?" asked Hannah. "Perhaps they weren't quite as smart as he thought they were. You know what parents are like."

"No one could believe their ears," said Mr. Rummage. "They made a fantastic impression. Everyone made a fuss of them and gave them candy and presents."

"Sounds as though they both got really spoiled," said Hannah.

"Well, it appears that Wolfgang did get quite excitable and a bit wild," Mr. Rummage explained.

"But so would I if I practiced for hours on end, had late nights, and was fed rich foods and candies around the clock," said Hannah.

"Wolfgang's dad said that although his son was playful and a bit naughty, he was always serious when he played the piano. So serious, in fact, that you couldn't joke with him or he'd have a tantrum."

"How sweet! Sounds likes someone else I know," said Hannah looking at her brother. "Hey, put that scratchy violin down—what a racket!"

European tour

In 1762, the Mozart children made a huge impression on the Bavarian court. During the next four years Leopold took the youngsters on European tours. They visited Vienna in 1763, and later toured London and Paris, where they played before royal families and dazzled their audiences.

Star performer

The children captivated the royal court of Vienna. Wolfgang showed how he could play difficult pieces at first sight, invent variations on a theme and even play blindfolded. The Empress Maria Theresa was so taken with the boy and he with her that he jumped up onto her lap and gave her a big hug. Then she presented him with a little gold-braided jacket to perform his concerts in.

Miracle children

One of the songs they performed was a kind of acrobatic piece where the pianist had to play on the keyboard with a cloth covering their fingers. No wonder they became known as miracle children. The critics wrote: "We can scarcely credit what we see with our own eyes and hear with our own ears." They played at royal courts, after which nobles rushed to invite them to perform in their stately homes and palaces. Gifts and money poured into Leopold's wallet, but the Mozarts moved on.

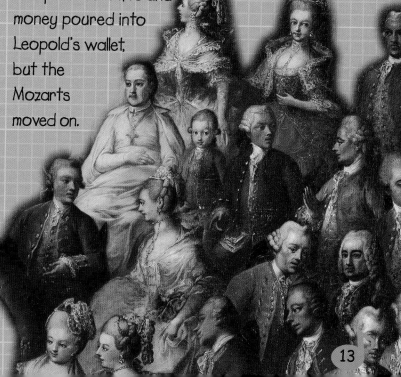

"Hi Chrissy," said Hannah to their friend from the Vintage Clothing stall. "What have you got there?"

"I heard you talking about my favorite composer, Mozart, and I just had to dig out these old clothes. They are the kind they wore in those days—aren't they fantastic?"

Digby's eyes lit up as he saw what was draped over Chrissy's arm. "Wow, can I try them on?"

"You certainly can," said Chrissy. "And I've got a wardrobe for Hannah as well."

"Oh what fun, a dressing up party," enthused Kenzo. "Now you wait right here. I have some very special wigs that you must try on. And they're just sooo… you, Hannah."

While Kenzo rushed off to get the wigs, Digby took a fine pair of silk, ivory-colored **breeches** and ducked behind the stall to put them on. Then he struggled into a white frilly shirt.

"What's this?" he asked holding up a long piece of white cloth.

"Something to strangle you with," said Hannah, who hadn't quite entered into the spirit of things yet.

"It's a **cravat**," laughed Chrissy. "You tie it around your neck, like this," and she showed Digby how.

"Now for Miss Hannah," said Chrissy, holding up a stiff **petticoat** and a gown with tucks and flounces.

"Oh, do I have to?" pouted Hannah.

"Of course you do, my dear," said Kenzo, who'd returned with what looked like a pile of bird's nests. "And look what I've got for you." Kenzo held up a white object that might have been cotton candy with a sailing ship perched on top. "Isn't this a simply divine creation?"

"How do I look?" asked Digby. "Hey, you look great, a real 18th century gentleman," said Chrissy.

"Wow, he looks almost respectable for once," said Hannah. "But how about this…" And she stepped forward, doing a twirl.

"Gorgeous," beamed Kenzo, as he placed a beehive wig on Hannah's head. "Well, look at you two! Wolfgang and Nannerl have come to life. Now go and sit at that old piano. I want to take a photo."

So, arm in arm, Wolfgang and Nannerl walked to the old piano at the side of Mr. Rummage's stall and sat down.

"It must have been great fun wearing glittering costumes, riding in carriages, and meeting royalty," said Digby.

"I expect it was certainly good at times, but there were probably some drawbacks," said Mr. Rummage.

"I can't see how," said Hannah, enjoying her role as a fashionable lady.

"Well, you'd have known about the drawbacks if you got sick in those days," said Mr. Rummage. "Everything was fine if you were healthy but if not, things were tough. Don't forget, this was a time when many children didn't survive to adulthood, and if you got a disease, such as smallpox, your chances of survival were really slim."

"Did Wolfgang get sick?" asked Hannah.

"Yes. The strain of touring Europe did take its toll on the children who were often ill. And after a bout of smallpox, Wolfgang was often weak and sickly," explained Mr. Rummage.

"Leopold sounds very cruel," said Hannah, "he made his children work so hard."

"Not really," said Mr. Rummage. "In those days it wasn't unusual for prodigies to be taken on a tour. Besides, Leopold always planned a few days rest between performances."

"He made a lot of money out of them, though, didn't he?" asked Digby.

"Up to a point, but like most parents, he wanted his children to have a secure future. Besides, he was convinced that showing off their talents to the world was a way of thanking God for their **genius**."

 # On the road

After the Mozarts' successful first tour, the family returned home a little better off than they were before. Leopold was able to buy his own carriage, but traveling was always a difficult business. The roads were bumpy and the carriage was cramped and cold. Wolfgang often passed the time thinking up tunes, which he would keep in his head until he had a chance to write them down.

Homesick boy

While he was traveling, Wolfgang made up a make-believe land called "Back," where children were always good and happy. He was king. This may have been because he was homesick and far away from his mother who always stayed at home. He even asked a family servant to draw a map of the land and made up names for the cities, villages, and markets. On one journey, Leopold wrote to his wife telling her that Wolfgang was cutting a new tooth—reminding us of just how young the boy was—not yet seven years old.

Genius composer

People were amazed at how quickly Wolfgang picked up anything to do with music. He composed his first symphony in 1764 when he was eight and his first **opera** in 1768 when he was just 12. By the time he was 13, he had written more than 80 pieces of music, including six symphonies. Mozart could compose complicated pieces without crossing things out or ever having second thoughts about it. He never made the same mistake twice, or ever repeated himself.

At the opera

Wolfgang's first love was opera. Even at a very young age he wanted to stage his own compositions. He loved the theater and was a pretty good actor. He also liked working with the artists. Unfortunately his first opera, *Ideomeno*, was not a hit. Some of the singers had not even set foot on a stage before, let alone performed an opera. Wolfgang complained that they just stood there like statues, and would not listen to his instructions.

Salieri the rival

Antonio Salieri, the Kapellmeister, or choirmaster, at the Viennese Court was a very popular composer who produced what people wanted to hear. Salieri's opera *Axur* was performed 100 times in public while Wolfgang's *Don Giovanni* was only performed nine times. This made Wolfgang jealous.

Duel of the operas

In 1761, Mozart and Salieri competed in a music contest held in the banqueting hall of the Schonbrunn Palace—Emperor Franz Joseph's summer home. Mozart's opera was performed at one end of the hall, Salieri's opera was staged at the other, and dinner was served in the middle. The sumptuous hall was so huge that the last notes echoed for five or six seconds after the music had stopped. Unfortunately Mozart lost the contest. He blamed the librettist: the person who wrote the words to the opera. The Emperor said he had used too many notes. Mozart angrily replied that he had used only as many as were necessary!

"Wolfgang wasn't always sick, was he?" asked Digby.

"No," smiled Mr. Rummage. "Mozart was able to carry on creating music until he'd become one of the greatest composers of his time—or any other time."

"Did people wait for his next composition just like people wait for a new record from a pop star today?" Hannah wanted to know.

"Not everyone liked what he wrote," answered Mr. Rummage. "Wolfgang's ideas were often considered too modern for the times and didn't catch on immediately—and then there was Salieri."

"Who was Salieri?" asked Hannah.

"Antonio Salieri was another composer," said Mr. Rummage. "He was also the court choirmaster of the Emperor, Joseph II in Vienna. Wolfgang first fell out with Salieri when Salieri was appointed music teacher to the Princess Elisabeth, even though Wolfgang had been recommended for the job. Wolfgang then criticized one of Salieri's operas as a 'wretched work.' From then on they were ready for an argument."

"Did anyone else like Salieri's operas?" asked Digby.

"Unfortunately the Emperor did. He liked operas to be serious—while Mozart's had a lot of dancing in them and made fun

of the nobility. Leopold advised his son to write in the popular style the Germans liked, but Wolfgang was determined to go his own way."

"Good for him," said Kenzo. "Well yes, except that Wolfgang wasn't very good with people, and in the end, he couldn't cope with all the arguments and plotting that went on at the Viennese court," said Mr. Rummage.

"He had plenty of work, to keep him occupied, didn't he?" asked Digby.

"Not really. Don't forget, he was no longer the prodigy who'd attracted big audiences as a child. He wanted to be in Vienna but now he couldn't find work there, so he went back to Salzburg."

"Well, at least he was back home. That must have made him happy," said Hannah.

"Actually, this was the start of a ten year period of unhappy and frustrating work under the Archbishop of Salzburg. So Wolfgang wasn't happy. Quite the opposite."

"Sounds really boring—I mean, working for an archbishop doesn't sound like a bundle of fun," said Digby, scratching his head under the wig he was wearing.

"He was treated like a servant and forced to compose music for processions, church services, weddings, and funerals," said Mr. Rummage. "It was a lot of hard work—hours of scratching away at manuscripts by candlelight."

"Sounds sort of romantic," said Hannah.

"It might have been," replied Mr. Rummage, "if Wolfgang had used wax candles. They were expensive, so he had to burn tallow ones made of animal fat and these smelled bad. Plus the work was tough. He had to write out the parts for every instrument in the orchestra. The Archbishop always wanted new stuff for every church service, so Wolfgang might only have a day to write a piece that had to be performed that night. Once, he composed six symphonies in three weeks."

"It does sound a bit hectic, but I suppose it was a steady job," said Hannah.

"It was, and Wolfgang wasn't easy to please. All that praise and pampering as a child had gone to his head. His father told him to be polite and concentrate on making a living, but Wolfgang wanted to be a star again, and dreamed of the golden opportunities he thought he could have if he returned to Vienna."

Master of dance

Wolfgang came back to Salzburg to compose and to conduct the court orchestra. But he began to hate his employer, who cruelly refused to let him play before the Emperor. Eventually, the Archbishop decided enough was enough and in 1781 he fired Wolfgang. Wolfgang was not too upset. He settled down and made a reasonable living by publishing his music and playing to the public. He was often asked to write dance music for balls and operas, which he loved doing.

Tour with mom

Wolfgang's mother did not tour with her son very often, but in 1777 she joined him on a visit to Mannheim and Paris. She was cheerful and hearty, but during the tour she became ill and died on July 3, 1778–probably of typhus fever. Wolfgang's great faith in God made it easier for him to accept her death. He wrote: "…we shall see her again …we shall live together far more happily and blissfully than ever in this world."

First love

From time to time Wolfgang went to stay with his friends: the Weber family. There he met and fell madly in love with Aloysia Weber, especially after hearing her beautiful singing voice. Leopold did not approve of the family, and was not at all pleased with this turn of events. However, he did not have to worry–Aloysia was not interested in young Wolfgang and rejected him.

Wedding bells

In 1782, Wolfgang married Constanze Weber, the little sister of his first love, Aloysia. His father disapproved, but they were an affectionate and happy couple who chatted a great deal, and had lots of friends. Constanze was not as talented as Wolfgang. She knew how to look after him though, and that was what he needed. She also bore him six children. The marriage was successful, although there was never enough money to go round.

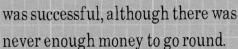

A happy home

Now back in Vienna, the Mozarts' little house was always noisy. Wolfgang was as playful and full of mischief as he had been as a boy. The rooms echoed to the sound of children playing. They had a pet dog, Guckel, and a caged starling that could whistle the theme from one of Wolfgang's piano concertos. However, most of the time, Wolfgang was hard at work—because of debt, the family had to move house eleven times in nine years!

"I bet Wolfgang didn't have to be that good-looking," said Hannah, "to have the pick of the girls."

"Well, he wasn't," said Mr. Rummage, "and yes, there were a few harmless flirtations, but he didn't believe in love affairs before marriage."

"So did he get married?" asked Digby.

"Yes," continued Mr. Rummage, "and would you believe it... he married Constanze, the younger sister of Aloysia Weber who'd been his first love."

"Was she beautiful?" asked Digby.

"Well, not exactly," said Mr. Rummage. "In fact, Wolfgang himself wrote:

'She is not ugly, but at the same time far from beautiful. Her whole beauty consists in two little black eyes and a pretty figure. She has no wit, but she has enough common sense to enable her to fulfil her duties as a wife and mother.'

"How rude!" said Hannah angrily. "I bet he didn't even love her."

"He did, but his father said she was unsuitable. Although she was a devoted wife, some people think that Mozart had to work hard to satisfy her expensive tastes." said Mr. Rummage.

"So a concerto might buy her a pair of shoes, a minuet a pair of gloves, and so on…"

"She had a go at Wolfgang too," said Kenzo huffily. "She told him he had to be a better businessman and take in more pupils—and she liked partying."

"But so did he," said Mr. Rummage. "In fact, they were as bad as each other.."

"So the Mozarts were back in Vienna," said Hannah. "That must have been nice. Mom is always saying Dad should take her there."

"Vienna was certainly a great place to live in Wolfgang's time," said Mr. Rummage. "It was home to the rich and influential people of the day—this was high society. Unfortunately, Wolfgang was only a poor musician, and musicians didn't have a good reputation in those days."

"Wolfgang liked Vienna. He drank coffee in the fashionable coffee houses, where he met important people who could get him more work. He wasn't always successful and people took advantage of him, often expecting him to compose for nothing."

Palace of Schonbrunn

The magnificent Schonbrunn Palace in Vienna was built to rival the Palace of Versailles belonging to the French kings. King Leopold I began the palace in 1695, but Empress Maria Theresa added the really grand bits. Of the 1441 rooms, some of the most magnificent were the **frescoed** audience rooms and gilded parlors of the Empress, where the six-year-old Wolfgang performed. One hall was hung with hundreds of mirrors and is called the *speigelsaal*, which means 'hall of mirrors' in German.

High society

Vienna was a city of beautiful palaces and gardens, ballrooms, opera houses, and coffee houses. It was a glittering and fashionable society where men and women wore expensive costumes and strutted about as if they were birds of paradise in full plumage. There were carnivals and masked balls too, which the Mozarts loved to attend. Wolfgang also enjoyed horseback riding in the magnificent parks and gardens. Unfortunately, by trying to keep up with their friends and put on a good show, the Mozarts spent more than they could afford.

Coffee houses

No one in Europe knew much about coffee before the 1600s. The drink first arrived in Vienna in 1683 after a war with the Turks when—as the story goes—an Austrian soldier found some Turkish coffee that had been left behind and opened the first Viennese coffee house. Mozart often visited these popular meeting places to relax and talk to friends and fellow musicians.

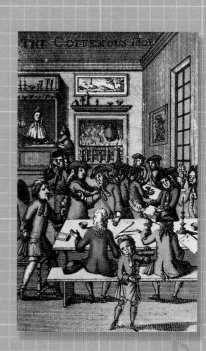

"How did Wolfgang survive if he worked for nothing?" asked Digby.

"That didn't happen often," said Mr. Rummage, "and he was generally quite well paid. He certainly wasn't as poor as some people have made him out to be—just careless with his money."

"How much did he earn?" asked Hannah.

"Wolfgang wrote to his father that he could make 1,000 gulden a year from a grand concert and four clavier pupils."

"What's a gulden?" asked Digby.

"It was a silver coin used at the time and worth about three American dollars," replied Mr. Rummage. "Then he had other performances and money from publishing his music. All in all, he probably earned about 4,000 gulden a year. A teacher earned just 100 gulden, so you can see he wasn't badly off at all."

"So where did the money go, then?" demanded Hannah.

"A lot went on shoes and clothing. Food was cheap, but taking care of your wig and pigtail wasn't. So he had to pay barbers as well as servants," said Mr. Rummage.

"He had servants?" asked Hannah.

"Well, that was normal in Vienna," said Mr. Rummage. "Extravagance was part of everyday life. It was the custom of gentlemen to wear a diamond ring on each little finger and carry two watches. But Wolfgang was also generous and very soft-hearted."

"A pushover, you mean," snorted Hannah. "There were plenty of 'false friends.' In fact, Wolfgang once loaned someone 300 gulden and never got it back. His pride made him keep his debts a secret. Worrying about money and working hard to pay off the bills was exhausting though, and in the end, his health suffered," said Mr. Rummage.

Unpopular opera

Wolfgang wrote at a fast pace. This was probably because most of the music he composed had been imagined and constructed in his mind long before he put **quill** to paper. The first part of his opera *Don Giovanni* was written after a party the night before the performance. *Don Giovanni* is one of Wolfgang's most popular operas, but it was not always so. It was not a success when it was staged in Vienna as it was thought to be too difficult.

Expensive vacation

In 1787, Wolfgang's father died. Then, two years later, Constanze became ill. Wolfgang sent her to a German spa, where she had to "take the waters" to recover. This was an expensive way to treat an illness and the composer had to take on more work to help pay the medical bills—at one point he owed 400 gulden to pharmacists. Also, Wolfgang was suffering from more illnesses, along with toothaches and headaches, and was becoming weaker. It did not stop him from writing, however.

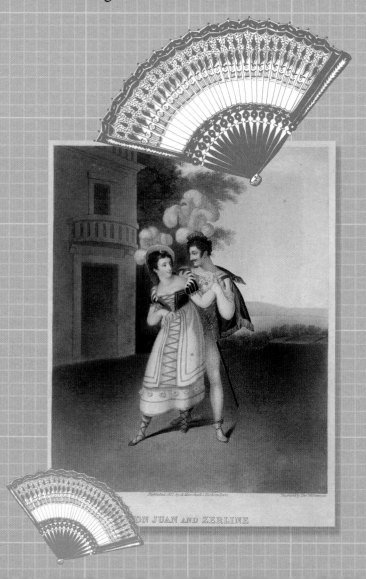

DON JUAN AND ZERLINE

"Despite illness and debt, Wolfgang enjoyed life and had lots of hobbies," said Mr. Rummage.

"Hobbies," said Digby, intrigued, "you mean like butterfly collecting?"

"Or knitting?" giggled Hannah.

"Not quite," said Mr. Rummage. "Wolfgang enjoyed *Bolzischiessen*.

"What's that?" cried the children.

"It was a kind of crossbow shooting." grinned Mr. Rummage. "The Mozarts belonged to the Bolt-Marksmen's Company in Salzburg. They shot air guns loaded with bolts—a kind of short arrow —at targets. The targets were often decorated with funny pictures. Wolfgang's were sometimes rude."

"Wow!" said Digby, "that sounds cool."

"He also belonged to a secret society," Mr. Rummage whispered behind his hand.

"Did he spy on people?" asked Digby expectantly. "No, it wasn't that kind of society. Wolfgang was a Freemason. He belonged to a Masonic Lodge."

"Aren't masons people who build walls?" asked Hannah.

"No, nothing like that," replied Mr. Rummage. "Freemasonry, as it's called, goes back hundreds of years.

Its members supposedly know secrets that no one else does. Wolfgang probably joined to make new friends, although Freemasons were often influential people and they would have helped his career."

"What were the secrets?" asked Digby

"They're secret," scowled Hannah. "If we knew them then they wouldn't be secret, would they?"

"Anyway," continued Mr. Rummage, "Wolfgang liked the Freemasons and even put some of their ideas into his opera, *The Magic flute*."

 # Secret society

Wolfgang composed music for a secret society, called the Freemasons. Emanuel Schikaneder, a theater manager and actor who wrote the words for *The Magic Flute*, was one. He and Wolfgang worked together to include the Masonic ideas of virtue, or goodness, into the opera. Another Freemason, Michael Puchberg, lent Mozart money when he asked for it. Puchberg was a wealthy merchant who helped the family out when Constanze became ill. But, unfortunately, Mozart died before he could repay his friend.

WOLFGANG WROTE A FANTASY FOR THE BARREL OF A MUSICAL CLOCK.

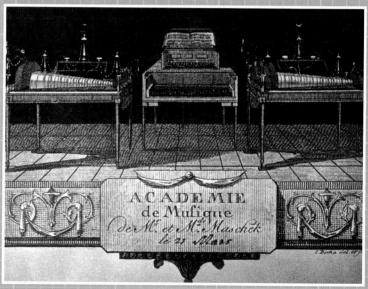

ACADEMIE
de Musique

MOZART WAS FASCINATED BY THE GLASS HARMONICA AND WROTE A PIECE ESPECIALLY FOR IT.

"The more Mozart worked, the more exhausted he became," said Mr. Rummage. "This made him so weak that he fell ill. He seemed to know what was happening and just three months before he died he wrote:

'My end has come before I could profit from my talent.'"

"So he died," said Hannah quietly. "He just got weak and died."

"Some say he was poisoned." said Kenzo

"Poisoned!" cried Digby. "Why would anyone want to poison a genius?"

"Did he have enemies?" asked Hannah. "Oh, he certainly did," said Mr. Rummage. "But whether they would have stooped to murdering him is another thing. No, what's more likely is that he just worked himself too hard."

"Why couldn't he rest?" asked Digby.

"Because the more Wolfgang owed the more he had to work to pay it off, Digby," explained Mr. Rummage.

Murder mystery?

Poisoned!

As he became more and more ill, Wolfgang told Constanze that he was being poisoned. He remembered his dead father's letter that had warned him not to walk out alone and to trust no one. He also knew that he was working in a court society where intrigue and suspicion were everywhere. And although Wolfgang admitted that he was jealous of Salieri's popularity, he also said many times that Salieri could not be trusted.

Jealous composer?

The problem was that Salieri seemed to admire Mozart very much. He went to see all of Wolfgang's operas. And, as choirmaster, he had his orchestra perform Wolfgang's music at the Viennese court. He even taught Mozart's son after the composer had died. The mystery and intrigue caught people's imagination and Salieri's envy of Wolfgang's talent was the background for an opera by Rimsky-Korsakov. It was also the theme of the modern film *Amadeus*. It was rumored that Salieri confessed on his deathbed to poisoning Wolfgang. But we will never be absolutely sure, as Mozart's body has never been found.

Mozart's requiem

The man in black

One dark night, when Wolfgang was not feeling at his best, a stranger dressed in black knocked at the composer's door. Wolfgang opened the door and greeted the man, but the mysterious stranger would not give his name. He said that he had been sent to ask Wolfgang to compose a requiem, or funeral mass. Wolfgang agreed to compose the requiem, but the man in black returned again and again to hurry Wolfgang along.

Mozart's last words

Wolfgang was now seriously ill and he began to imagine things. He believed that he was writing the music for his own funeral. He would see the strange man at the door both in his dreams and while he was awake—almost as if he were urging the composer to finish before he died. Mozart desperately wanted to finish the requiem before his death. As he lay dying, he even mouthed the drum rolls to his pupil Sussmayer. But it was no use—he did not make it and Sussmayer had to finish the piece for him. Today, it is considered one of the most glorious pieces of music ever written.

"It must have been a real shock to see the strange figure at his door." said Mr. Rummage. "Wolfgang had no idea who or what it was."

"Spooky!" shuddered Digby. "Do you think he was a ghost?"

"No, silly," said Hannah, "there's no such thing as ghosts."

"Wolfgang probably thought it was," said Mr. Rummage. "Or perhaps he thought it was an angel of death."

"Now you're really scaring me," said Digby, with a shiver.

"I bet it was Salieri," said Hannah.

"Well, it was neither a ghost nor Salieri," said Mr. Rummage. "We now know that the man in black was the servant of a count. The count wanted the music for his wife's funeral, but he also wanted to pass it off as his own. The trouble was that poor Wolfgang was so sick and feverish he probably couldn't think clearly."

"It's sad that Wolfgang died when he was so young," said Hannah. "Just think of all the beautiful music he might have composed if he'd lived longer."

"He could have bought a new wig as well. I bet there's all sorts of things under this one," said Digby taking it off to scratch his head again.

"Ah but it's a special wig," smiled Mr. Rummage. "Some people think that if you listen to Mozart's music it makes you smarter. You never know, every time you put on that wig, it might make you smarter too. You might even learn to play the piano."

"Huh! It'd have to be a very special wig to do that," said Hannah.

"It is," said Digby indignantly, "and one day I might even compose something."

"You'll need more than a wig to do that," said Hannah, still giggling as she led Digby and his wig away from Mr. Rummage's stall. "Bye, see you next Saturday, Mr. Rummage."

Mozart's legacy

Mozart died in 1791 at the age of only 35. But his music lives on. He composed over 600 works, including 21 stage and opera works, 15 masses, over 50 symphonies, 25 piano concertos, 12 violin concertos, 27 concert arias, 17 piano sonatas, 26 string quartets, and many other pieces. His style was unique and unlike many of the musical styles of his day. Sadly, most people did not appreciate his music while he was alive. They did not understand his complex and extraordinary talent.

ONLY TWO OF MOZART'S CHILDREN SURVIVED. FRANCE XAVIER WOLFGANG, WHO BECAME A MUSICIAN LIKE HIS FATHER, AND KARL THOMAS.

The work of a genius

Mozart's music has remained popular ever since his death. People like it because it sparkles with melodies that they can remember. Most of us recognize his *Eine Kleine Nachtmusik*, the Concerto no. 21 and his symphony no. 40, even if we do not know their names. He has written some of the most popular operas as well. His *The Magic Flute* and *Marriage of Figaro* are still loved for their fun factor and the musical magic that Mozart constructed around the stories. Mozart insisted that music was the essence of his operas and they certainly are. No generation has ever tired of Mozart, and his music is as fresh now as the day he wrote it.

Glossary

breeches Short pants for males that end just below the knee

clavier A musical instrument played by a keyboard and resembling a piano

composer A person who creates music. The music created is called a composition

concerto A piece of classical music written to be performed with opportunities for solo instruments, and to be accompanied by an orchestra

cravat A scarf or neckband fashionable for males in the 1700's

duet Music to be performed by two musicians

frescoed A method of painting on freshly plastered walls, so that the image remains forever

genius An exceptional abilty, or a person who possesses exceptional ability

harpsichord An early musical instrument played by a keyboard and resembling a piano

opera A play set to music performed by singers and musicians

petticoat A girl's or woman's undergarment shaped like a skirt and to be worn underneath dresses

pomades Scented ointment used to shape and hold hair styles

prodigy A young and exceptionally talented person

quill A writing instrument made from a hallow bird's feather. The sharpened end was dipped in ink and used as a pen

Index

Other characters in the Stories of Great People series.

SAFFRON sells pots and pans, herbs, spices, oils, soaps, and dyes from her spice kitchen set up under under a shady awning.

BUZZ is a street vendor with all the gossip. He sells candies from a tray that's strapped around his neck.

COLONEL KARBUNCLE sells military uniforms, medals, flags, swords, helmets, cannon balls—all from the trunk of his old jeep.

Mrs. BILGE pushes her cleaning cart around the market, picking up garbage. Trouble is, she's always throwing away the objects on Mr. Rummage's stall.

Mr. CLUMPMUGGER has an amazing collection of ancient maps, dusty books, and old newspapers in his rare prints stall.

YOUSSEF has traveled to many places around the world. He carries a bag full of souvenirs from his exciting journeys.